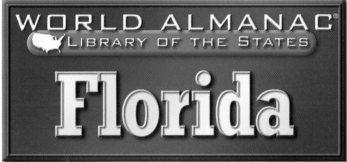

THE SUNSHINE STATE

by Patricia Chui

Curriculum Consultant: Jean Craven,
Director of Instructional Support,
Albuquerque, NM, Public Schools

WORLD ALMANAC® LIBRARY

Please visit our web site at: www.worldalmanaclibrary.com
For a free color catalog describing World Almanac® Library's list of high-quality books
and multimedia programs, call 1-800-848-2928 or fax your request to (414) 332-3567.

Library of Congress Cataloging-in-Publication Data

Chui, Patricia.
    Florida, the Sunshine State / by Patricia Chui.
       p. cm. — (World Almanac Library of the states)
    Includes bibliographical references and index.
    Summary: Illustrations and text present the history, geography, people,
politics and government, economy, and social life and customs of Florida.
    ISBN 0-8368-5114-5 (lib. bdg.)
    ISBN 0-8368-5283-4 (softcover)
    1. Florida—Juvenile literature. [1. Florida.] I. Title. II. Series.
F311.3.C48   2002
975.9—dc21   2001046991

This edition first published in 2002 by
World Almanac® Library
330 West Olive Street, Suite 100
Milwaukee, WI 53212 USA

This edition © 2002 by World Almanac® Library.

Design and Editorial: **Jack&Bill**/Bill SMITH STUDIO Inc.
Editors: Jackie Ball and Kristen Behrens
Art Directors: Ron Leighton and Jeffrey Rutzky
Photo Research and Buying: Christie Silver and Sean Livingstone
Design and Production: Maureen O'Connor and Jeffrey Rutzky
World Almanac® Library Editors: Patricia Lantier, Amy Stone, Valerie J. Weber,
Catherine Gardner, Carolyn Kott Washburne, Alan Wachtel, Monica Rausch
World Almanac® Library Production: Scott M. Krall, Eva Erato-Rudek, Tammy Gruenewald

Photo credits: p. 4 © Corel; p. 6 (left) © Corel, (top and bottom right) © PhotoDisc; p. 7 (top)
© PhotoDisc, (bottom) © Andrew McCloskey/TimePix; p. 9 © Corel; p. 10 © Christie K Silver;
p. 11 © Dover Publications; p. 12 © Francis Miller/TimePix; p. 13 © Dover Publications; p. 14
postcard © Lake County Museum/CORBIS; p. 14 (top) © Corbis, © Lake County Museum,
(bottom) © Library of Congress; p. 15 © Colin Braley/TimePix; p. 17 © Corel; p. 18 (top)
© Ricky Rogers/TimePix, (bottom), © PhotoDisc; p. 20 (all) courtesy of Visit Florida; p. 21 (from
left to right) courtesy of Visit Florida; courtesy of Visit Florida; © Corel; p. 22 (from left to right)
NASA, © Yale Joel/TimePix; p. 27 © PhotoDisc; p. 29 courtesy of Tallahassee CVB; p. 30
courtesy of Tallahassee CVB; p. 31 © Marc Serota/TimePix; p. 32 © Corel; p. 33 © Corel;
p. 34 © Corel; p. 35 © Jim Bourg/TimePix; p. 36 (top) © ArtToday, (bottom) © Corel; p. 37
© Bettmann/CORBIS; p. 39 © Francis Miller/TimePix; p. 40 © PhotoDisc; p. 41 © Yale
Joel/TimePix; p. 42–43 © Library of Congress; p. 44 (clockwise) © Corel, © Corel,
© PhotoDisc; p. 45 (top) © ArtToday, (bottom) © Nik Wheeler/CORBIS

Printed in the United States of America

1 2 3 4 5 6 7 8 9 06 05 04 03 02

Florida

Sun, Moon, and a Mouse

There's lots of sun in Florida — what else would you expect from a place called the Sunshine State? In Florida, however, you can also reach the moon. Florida is home to the Kennedy Space Center, the launching site for U.S. missions to outer space. The stars are within reach, too. A certain celebrity mouse who hangs out in Orlando has made Disney World and its related theme parks the world's biggest attraction.

People flock to Florida to visit Mickey Mouse and friends but also to swim, surf, snorkel, fish, and play golf or tennis. The state's recreational opportunities are matchless, especially for water sports. Most of Florida is a peninsula, a finger of land surrounded on three sides by water. This, combined with its warm, semitropical climate, spells "vacation."

Birds flock here, too — exotic pelicans, flamingos, and roseate spoonbills. Millions of butterflies migrate, just like vacationers and retirees, to escape the wintry north. Flowers, fruits, and vegetables grow year-round, perhaps why Ponce de León picked the name *florida* — Spanish for "flowery" — when he explored the area in 1513.

Spanish heritage, tradition, and culture still dominate parts of Florida, especially the Miami area where the Cuban-American population is as large as 40 percent. It began to swell in the 1960s as Cuban refugees fled Fidel Castro's government. Florida also made headlines in 2000 when another Cuban refugee, a boy named Elián Gonzalez, became the focus of an international tug-of-war. Later that year the state made headlines in an entirely different way as electoral votes were disputed in the closest presidential race in history. Somehow Florida continues to be both a vibrant place that plays an influential part in the bustle of everyday U.S. life and a relaxing tropical haven for those who want to get away from it all.

▶ Map of Florida showing interstate highway system, as well as major cities and waterways.

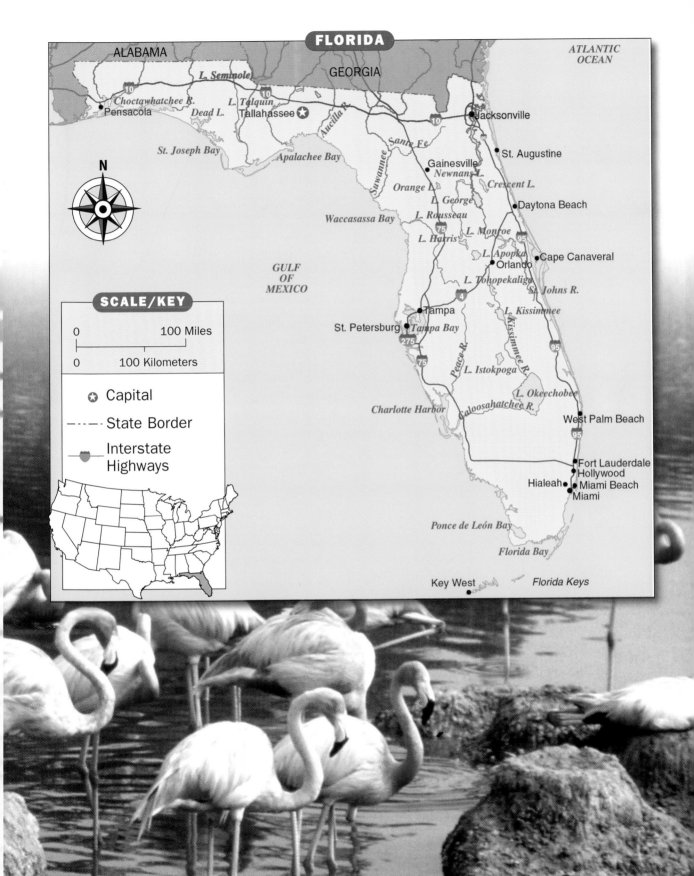

FLORIDA

ALABAMA

GEORGIA

ATLANTIC OCEAN

L. Seminole

Choctawhatchee R.
Pensacola
Dead L.
L. Talquin
Tallahassee ✪

Aucilla R.

Jacksonville

St. Joseph Bay

Apalachee Bay

Santa Fe

St. Augustine

Suwannee R.

Gainesville
Newnans L.

Orange L.

Crescent L.

Daytona Beach

L. George

Waccasassa Bay

L. Rousseau

L. Monroe

N

L. Harris

L. Apopka
Orlando

Cape Canaveral

GULF
OF
MEXICO

L. Tohopekaliga

St. Johns R.

Tampa

L. Kissimmee

St. Petersburg
Tampa Bay

Peace R.

L. Istokpoga

L. Okeechobee

West Palm Beach

Charlotte Harbor

Caloosahatchee R.

Fort Lauderdale
Hollywood
Hialeah
Miami Beach
Miami

Ponce de León Bay

Florida Bay

Key West
Florida Keys

SCALE/KEY

0   100 Miles

0   100 Kilometers

✪ Capital

---·--- State Border

Interstate Highways

Fast Facts

Florida (FL), The Sunshine State

Entered Union
March 3, 1845 (27th state)

Capital — **Population**
Tallahassee 150,624

Total Population (2000)
15,982,378 (4th largest in the U.S.)

Largest Cities — **Population**
Jacksonville 735,617
Miami 362,470
Tampa 303,447
St. Petersburg 248,232

Land Area
53,927 square miles (139,671 square kilometers) (26th largest state)

State Motto
"In God We Trust"

State Song
"The Swanee River" ("Old Folks at Home") *by Stephen C. Foster*

State Animal
Florida panther

State Saltwater Mammal
Porpoise

State Bird
Mockingbird

State Marine Mammal
Manatee

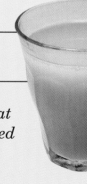

State Fish
Largemouth bass

State Saltwater Fish
Sailfish

State Insect
Zebra longwing butterfly — *This butterfly feeds only on the flowers of passionflowers.*

State Reptile
Alligator

State Tree
Sabal palmetto palm

State Flower
Orange blossom

State Shell
Horse conch

State Gem
Moonstone — *Although the state gem commemorates the July 20, 1969, moon landing by Neil Armstrong and Buzz Aldrin, this gemstone is neither native to Florida nor found on the moon.*

State Beverage
Orange juice

State Day
April 2 — *The approximate day that Ponce de León sighted Florida in 1513.*

PLACES TO VISIT

Walt Disney World *Orlando*
Four separate theme parks make up Florida's most popular attraction: The Magic Kingdom Park, Disney's Animal Kingdom Park, Disney-MGM Studios, and Epcot Center. The parks feature amusement rides, exhibits, live entertainment, Disney characters, and tours.

Kennedy Space Center *Cape Canaveral*
Started in 1962 as part of the U.S. space program, this vast complex is now the launch site for the space shuttle. The center's vehicle assembly building, where rockets and shuttles are put together, is one of the largest buildings in the world.

Everglades National Park
The park encompasses most of Florida's southern tip as well as Florida Bay. A region of wetlands, cypress swamps, and pine forests, the park is also the only place on Earth where alligators and crocodiles live side by side.

For other places and events, see p. 44

BIGGEST, BEST, AND MOST

- St. Augustine is the oldest continuously occupied European settlement in North America. Spanish soldiers established a fort on the site in 1565.

- The Seven Mile Bridge connects the Middle Keys to the Lower Keys and is the longest segmental bridge in the world.

- The most theme parks in one city can be found in Orlando, home of Disney World, Seaworld, and Universal Studios.

STATE FIRSTS

- 1539 — Explorer Hernando de Soto sent a report of his voyage back to the king of Spain, becoming the first person to send a letter from North America.

- 1962 — Astronaut John Glenn became the first American to orbit Earth when his rocket was launched from Cape Canaveral.

Best Desserts

Florida is famous for Key lime pie. The classic recipe uses a filling made from the tart juice of Key limes topped with meringue and baked in a graham cracker crust. The first Key lime pies were made in Key West, the outermost island of the Florida Keys. Despite their name, Key limes are not native to Key West. Instead, they were brought over by tradesmen from the Caribbean in the 1500s. Every year Key West hosts the Key Lime Festival, in which local restaurants and bakeries hold a contest for the most delicious Key lime pie.

"For that Deep-Down Body Thirst"

In 1965 Robert Cade, a professor at the University of Florida Medical School, developed a sports drink that was tested with ten of the school's football players. The hot Florida sun made play and practice especially challenging, and something was needed to keep the players strong and hydrated. The drink was called Gatorade, after the school's mascot. A Miami reporter covered one of the games and asked what had been in all the empty drink cartons; when told that it was a new sports drink designed for vigorous exercise, he wrote a story about it in the *Miami Herald.* That story and others launched the drink to national prominence. Today Cade's invention is popular worldwide, bringing in almost $2 billion a year in revenue to its parent company, Quaker Oats.

Land of Many Flags

> It is a thing unspeakable to consider the things that be seen there, and shall be found more and more in this incomparable land, which, never yet broken with plough irons, bringeth forth all things according to its first nature, wherewith the eternal God endowed it.
>
> — *Jean Ribault,* The Whole and True Discoverye of Terra Florida

The First Floridians

Florida's earliest inhabitants most likely migrated across North America to the Florida peninsula more than ten thousand years ago, probably following such big game as mammoths, mastodons, and saber-toothed tigers. Florida's varied environments, capable of supporting many different forms of plant and animal life, may have also attracted these first settlers. After big-game animals became extinct at the end of the most recent ice age, about ten thousand years ago, the people relied on small-game animals, shellfish, plants, and nuts for their food. They also cultivated crops of corn, beans, and squash.

Five major tribes dominated Florida by the time the first Europeans arrived in the sixteenth century. The total Native population in Florida may have been as high as four hundred thousand, but this number would soon drop sharply. Large numbers of Native Americans in Florida fell victim to European diseases such as influenza, measles, and smallpox. War and enslavement also took their toll.

Native Americans of Florida
Apalachee
Ais
Calusa
Creek
Mikasusi
Seminole
Tequesta
Timucua

An Explorer's Prize

The country where we came on shore to this town and region of Apalachen is for the most part level, the ground of sand and stiff earth. . . . There are many lakes, great and small, over every part of it.
— Cabeza de Vaca, survivor of Panfilo de Narváez's voyage, reporting to the king of Spain, 1542

The first European to reach Florida was the Spanish

▲ Typical tropical scene in southern Florida.

explorer Juan Ponce de León. Thinking Florida was an island, he came ashore in 1513 and gave the territory its name. Other Spanish explorers followed. In 1528 Panfilo de Narváez led an expedition of four hundred men to Florida's southwestern coast, but most of the company perished in a shipwreck. Hernando de Soto came to Florida in 1539, exploring the peninsula and surrounding areas. For five months he camped in northern Florida. De Soto was the leader of the first European expedition to reach the Mississippi River, where he died in 1542.

Twenty years later the French made their own attempt to

DID YOU KNOW?

Álvar Nuñez Cabeza de Vaca, a member of Narvaéz company, was the first African known to have touched shore in Florida.

establish a foothold in the region. In 1562 a group of Huguenots (French Protestants) led by Jean Ribault claimed St. Johns River for France before sailing north to form a colony in what is now South Carolina. Two years later René Goulaine de Laudonnière returned to establish Fort Caroline at the river's mouth, near present-day Jacksonville.

King Philip II of Spain, alarmed at the French presence in the area, sent Captain Pedro Menéndez de Avilés to Florida in 1565 with instructions to drive out the French. On his arrival Menéndez founded St. Augustine. With a force of more than one thousand men and ten ships, Menéndez captured Fort Caroline, renaming it San Mateo. Almost all of the French settlers were massacred, including Jean Ribault.

The Spanish, French, and soon the British continued to compete for the territory. Frenchman Dominique de Gourgues recaptured San Mateo in 1567; British captain Sir Francis Drake looted and burned St. Augustine in 1586. By 1600, however, the Spanish presence in Florida was firmly established.

In the mid-1700s, the Seven Years' War broke out among

▶ Castillo de San Marcos (in English, Saint Mark's Fort), built from 1672 to 1695. The fort guarded St. Augustine, the first permanent European settlement in what would eventually become the continental United States. Today Castillo de San Marcos is a national landmark.

the European nations. (The French and Indian War was part of that conflict.) Spain and France sided together against Great Britain. At the 1763 Treaty of Paris, which concluded the war, Spain gave Florida to Britain in exchange for Havana, Cuba.

The Contest for Florida

His Catholic Majesty cedes to the United States, in full property and sovereignty, all the territories which belong to him, situated to the Eastward of the Mississippi, known by the name of East and West Florida.
— from the Adams-Onis Treaty of 1821

The British divided Florida into two colonies: East Florida and West Florida. Britain controlled both colonies for about twenty years, until the Revolutionary War. During that conflict East and West Florida remained loyal to Britain, but Spain captured West Florida in 1781. The 1783 Treaty of Paris, which ended the Revolutionary War, returned the rest of Florida to Spanish control once more.

Spanish rule was a troubling time for Florida. It was the only territory in southeastern North America that did not belong to the newly created United States. Border disputes broke out frequently. The region's population changed, as most British colonists left to resettle in the British-controlled West Indies. Florida's population came to consist of Spanish settlers and the runaway slaves and prisoners who took refuge there.

During the War of 1812, Spain allowed Great Britain to use Pensacola as a base. U.S. general Andrew Jackson captured Pensacola in 1814, returning in 1818 to defeat the Native Americans fighting for the British in a conflict known as the First Seminole War. Although Jackson's unauthorized actions brought the United States to the brink of war with both Britain and Spain, Secretary of State John Quincy Adams was able to keep the peace. In the Adams-Onis Treaty of 1819, Spain reluctantly ceded Florida to the United States in exchange for $5 million in property damages.

In Search of the Fountain of Youth

Juan Ponce de León (1460–1521) was a Spanish nobleman and explorer. Many historians believe that he sailed on Christopher Columbus's second voyage to the West Indies in 1493. After expeditions to Hispaniola (now Haiti and the Dominican Republic) and Puerto Rico, de León set off again. He may have been headed for Bimini, an island north of Cuba. Some say he hoped to find the legendary Fountain of Youth but others believe he was looking for riches. Instead, de León landed on the northeast coast of Florida, near what is now St. Augustine, just after Easter in 1513. He claimed the land for Spain and named it *Florida* in honor of Spain's Easter celebration, *Pascua Florida* ("feast of the flowers"). De León returned to Florida in 1521 with 250 people and fifty horses, but his colonization attempt failed when the expedition was attacked by Native Americans. De León was wounded and died shortly afterward in Cuba.

Expelling the Seminoles

The tract you have ceded will soon be surveyed and sold, and immediately afterwards will be occupied by a white population. You will soon be in a state of starvation. . . . You will be resisted, punished, perhaps killed. Now, is it not better peaceably to remove to a fine, fertile country, occupied by your own kindred, and where you can raise all the necessaries of life, and where game is yet abundant? . . . You have no right to stay, and you must go.

— President Andrew Jackson, address to Seminole chiefs, February 16, 1835

Andrew Jackson was named Florida's provisional governor in 1821 and charged with setting up a territorial government. In 1822 Congress organized the official Territory of Florida, naming William P. Duval as its first governor and designating Tallahassee as the capital.

Almost immediately conflicts arose between the new settlers pouring into the region and Native people. The Spanish referred to the various Native American tribes in Florida as Seminoles, possibly a corruption of the Spanish word *cimarrones,* meaning "wild people" or "runaways." The non-European population in the 1700s and early 1800s consisted of members of Florida's original tribes, Creek

▼ A Seminole family in Big Cypress, circa 1949.

Indians who had migrated from Georgia and Alabama, and runaway slaves who lived among the Native Americans.

Both as a military leader and later as president, Jackson played a major role in negotiating treaties that stripped Native Americans of their lands in exchange for territory further west. In 1830 President Jackson pushed Congress to pass the Indian Removal Act, under which treaties were negotiated that required all Native American tribes east of the Mississippi River to relocate into what is now Oklahoma. Some Native Americans accepted the terms peacefully, but most of the Seminoles resisted, giving rise to the Second Seminole War (1835–1842). This was the longest, most expensive war the U.S. government would ever wage against Native Americans. At a cost of more than $20 million and the lives of more than fifteen hundred soldiers, the United States won. Most of the surviving Seminoles were relocated to Oklahoma.

The Third Seminole War (1855–1858) erupted after Seminole leader Holata Micco, provoked by U.S. soldiers, led his followers into action against his attackers. When the war was over, only approximately two hundred Seminoles remained in Florida. Most of these moved to the Everglades to live in hiding.

Statehood

We, the People of the State of Florida in Convention assembled, do solemnly ordain, publish and declare: That the State of Florida hereby withdraws herself from the Confederacy of States existing under the name of the United States of America, and from the existing Government of said States; and that all political connection between her and the Government of said States ought to be and the same is hereby totally annulled.
— Ordinance of Secession, January 10, 1861

On March 3, 1845, Florida became the twenty-seventh state in the Union, admitted as a slave-holding state with a population of about sixty-eight thousand people. William D. Moseley, a lawyer from North Carolina, was the state's first governor.

When Abraham Lincoln was elected president in 1860, slave states felt threatened by the antislavery views of the North. On January 10, 1861, Florida became the third state

▲ Seminole leader Holata Micco, also known as Billy Bowlegs, fought long and hard to keep his peoples' land. At that time the United States was offering bounty hunters money for the capture of Seminoles — $500 for men, $250 for women, and $100 for children. Seminoles could receive the same amount for giving themselves up. Holata Micco left the choice in the hands of each person, but when his granddaughter was seized, he surrendered and was relocated to "Indian Territory" in present-day Oklahoma. Holata Micco later fought in the Union Army in the Civil War as a member of the First Indian Regiment.

to secede from the Union, joining the Confederate States of America. During the Civil War, Union forces captured Florida's coastal towns, but the Confederates managed to retain control of the state's interior after the Battle of Olustee. Florida contributed fifteen thousand troops and supplies such as corn, molasses, cattle, and salt. By the war's end Tallahassee was one of only two Southern capitals to avoid Union capture. When the Confederacy surrendered, however, the city was occupied by federal troops and the state placed under military rule. After a new constitution was drafted granting African Americans the right to vote, Florida was readmitted to the Union in 1868.

An Age of Growth

The late 1800s were a period of accelerated growth for Florida. With the plantation economy in decline, Florida turned to new industries such as cattle raising, citrus farming, and phosphate mining. To help expand road and railroad construction, the Florida legislature passed legislation offering free or cheap public land to investors interested in transportation. In the 1880s and 1890s, businessman Henry Flagler developed the Florida East Coast Railway and a string of resort hotels, bringing rail service and tourists all the way down the Atlantic coast to Miami and Key West. Trains could also quickly transport fresh produce to northern cities from the south of Florida, where swamplands had been drained to make more land for farming.

▲ A Key West postcard, circa 1952.

The years between the end of World War I (1914–1918) and 1925 were a period of spectacular growth for Florida. Cars, resorts, and land development enabled more and more people to move to Florida. These glory days ended in 1926 when Florida was hit by a crippling economic depression. This was followed by hurricanes in 1926 and 1928 and a plague of fruit flies in 1929, all of which reduced citrus production by 60 percent. Shortly thereafter the entire nation was struck by the Great Depression.

▼ The Royal Palm Hotel, Miami, circa 1912.

World War II

Florida was a key state during World War II (1939–1945). Its mild climate was ideal for training U.S. armed forces, and its location along the Atlantic Ocean (and proximity to the Panama Canal) gave it strategic importance in the defense of the Western Hemisphere. Florida was home to numerous military bases, which contributed to another spurt of growth after the war. Newly constructed highways and airports, combined with the state's resources and climate, attracted more tourists. Florida also gained prominence in the fledgling U.S. aeronautics industry. In 1958 the launch of the first U.S. satellite, *Explorer I,* from Cape Canaveral helped establish Florida as a major center for space exploration.

Florida Today

Today Florida is the fourth most populous state in the nation. Retirees from all over move to the state because of its mild winter climate. Florida's proximity to Cuba and the Caribbean has also made it a destination for those seeking political asylum. The Cuban revolution in 1959 and the 1991 military coup in Haiti led several thousand refugees to flee their homelands and resettle in Miami and other cities.

Hurricane Andrew crippled much of southern Florida in August 1992, causing over $20 billion in damages, killing thirty-nine people, and leaving more than two hundred thousand without homes. It was the most expensive natural disaster in U.S. history.

Florida gained the national spotlight in the close presidential election of 2000, when the state's final vote tally was disputed. The outcome of the election was delayed for a month while more than one hundred thousand ballots were disputed and recounted.

▲ Contested Florida ballots in the 2000 presidential election are examined by Democratic attorney Nicole Pillard and Florida Canvassing Board Chair Judge Charles Burton.

A Rich Tapestry

> If I had my way I'd always stay
> In Florida among the palms
>
> — *Irving Berlin*, In Florida Among the Palms,
> *Ziegfeld Follies (1916)*

Sixteen Million Strong and Growing

The 2000 census put Florida's population at almost sixteen million, a 23.5 percent increase over the previous census in 1990. The nation's fourth-largest state in population, Florida continues to attract new residents — whether old or young, U.S.- or foreign-born, seeking political asylum or simply some time in the sun. Most live in cities or towns, with 90 percent in Florida's twenty metropolitan areas. Florida's appeal as a retirement destination means the state's population is the oldest in the country. Almost 18 percent of Florida's residents are over sixty-five, which is 5 percent higher than the U.S. average.

Native Americans

With the arrival of Europeans in the 1500s, Florida's Native population was, over time, almost completely wiped out by

Age Distribution in Florida	
0–4	945,823
5–19	3,102,909
20–24	928,310
25–44	4,569,347
45–64	3,628,492
65 and over	2,807,497

Across One Hundred Years

Florida's three largest foreign-born groups for 1890 and 1990

1890			1990		
Cuba & West Indies 12,282	Norway & Denmark 1,855	Ireland 1,056	Cuba 497,619	Haiti 83,249	Jamaica 74,863

Total state population: 391,422
Total foreign-born: 22,932 (6%)

Total state population: 12,937,926
Total foreign-born: 1,662,601 (13%)

Patterns of Immigration

The total number of people who immigrated to Florida in 1998 was 59,965. Of that number, the largest immigrant groups were from Cuba (24%), Haiti (11%), and Jamaica (8%).

disease, slavery, and war. Meanwhile, Creek tribes from Georgia and Alabama were migrating to Florida. These Native groups were known collectively as the Seminoles.

A series of conflicts in the 1800s ravaged Florida's Native American population; most of the survivors relocated to Oklahoma. By the mid-1800s only several hundred Seminoles remained in Florida, isolated in the Everglades. Descendants of these people, numbering about three thousand, now live on reservations in Big Cypress, Brighton, Hollywood, Immokalee, and Tampa.

▲ Sunseekers at Clearwater Beach on Florida's west coast.

Heritage and Background, Florida   Year 2000

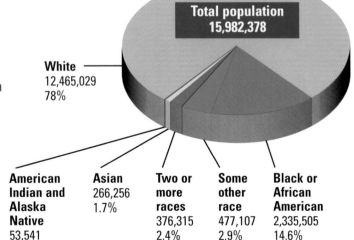

▶ Here's a look at the racial backgrounds of Floridians today. Florida ranks fourteenth among all U.S. states with regard to African Americans as a percentage of the population.

Total population 15,982,378

White 12,465,029 78%

Note: 16.8% (2,682,715) of the population identify themselves as **Hispanic** or **Latino**, a cultural designation that crosses racial lines. Hispanics and Latinos are counted in this category and the racial category of their choice.

Native Hawaiian and other Pacific Islander 8,625 0.1%

American Indian and Alaska Native 53,541 0.3%

Asian 266,256 1.7%

Two or more races 376,315 2.4%

Some other race 477,107 2.9%

Black or African American 2,335,505 14.6%

Europeans and Their Descendants

No sizable European population lived in Florida until the United States assumed control in 1822. In the early 1900s Florida experienced a commercial boom that attracted new residents from all over, including immigrants from Europe. The town of Tarpon Springs became a bustling Greek community around this time, where immigrants established a prosperous industry harvesting natural sponges. During World War I the cigar industry attracted immigrants from northern Spain, while a wave of Italians arrived after the war ended.

African Americans

In the 1600s and 1700s, Florida was a refuge for slaves fleeing plantations in neighboring southern states. Florida was not under U.S. control, so there was no system for enforcing slavery laws. By the time Florida became a state, almost all the state's African Americans were slaves. At the time they comprised about half of Florida's population.

The Civil War led to the emancipation of the slaves, but many African Americans continued to work on plantations as tenant farmers and sharecroppers. It was not until

The Battle over Elián

On November 25, 1999, six-year-old Elián Gonzalez was found clinging to an inner tube off the coast of Florida. His mother and ten others had drowned in an attempt to escape Cuba. Relatives in Miami took Elián in, while Fidel Castro and Elián's father (remarried and living in Havana) demanded the boy's return. The issue was finally resolved when federal agents raided the relatives' home and took the boy before dawn on April 22, 2000. Elián was eventually returned to his father.

▼ The skyline of Miami, one of Florida's liveliest vacation destinations.

Florida's phenomenal growth period at the turn of the twentieth century that the number of white residents increased faster than the number of African Americans.

Educational Levels of Florida Workers	
Less than 9th grade	842,811
9th to 12th grade, no diploma	1,428,263
High school graduate, including equivalency	2,679,285
Some college, no degree	1,723,385
Associate degree	589,019
Bachelor's degree	1,062,649
Graduate or professional degree	561,756

Religion

More than 80 percent of Florida's population is Christian. Florida's history as a Spanish colony, combined with immigrant populations from traditionally Roman Catholic countries are reflected in a Roman Catholic population of about 14 percent. Florida's largest Christian denomination, however, is Baptist — about 30 percent. Protestant denominations include Episcopalian (2.4 percent), United Methodist (3.6 percent), and Lutheran (approximately 4 percent). Not all Floridians are Christian, however. As many as 4.8 percent are Jewish, 2.4 percent are Muslim, and both Buddhists and Hindus make up about 0.1 percent of the population. One percent of Florida's population is agnostic, which means that they neither believe nor disbelieve in God.

Cuba and the Caribbean

Only 90 miles (145 kilometers) away, Cuba has had a significant impact on the history and people of Florida. Early Spanish explorers and traders en route to Florida used Cuba as a stopping point. The first wave of Cubans to move to Florida followed Vicente Martínez Ybor, a cigar entrepreneur who relocated his cigar factories from Havana to Key West, then to Tampa in 1886. When Cuba fell under communist control, about one hundred thousand Cuban exiles moved to Florida, most to the Miami area. Another surge of immigrants arrived in 1980, after Cuban leader Fidel Castro briefly opened the port of Mariel for emigration. Today there are half a million Cubans in Florida, many of whom maintain an active opposition to the Castro regime. Nearly one-third of foreign-born Floridians are from Cuba.

After a 1991 military coup in Haiti, thousands of Haitian refugees came to Florida. Miami — now home not only to Cubans and Haitians but also to Jamaicans, Puerto Ricans, Nicaraguans, Colombians, and Brazilians — has become the primary U.S. trade and transportation link to Latin America and the Caribbean.

The entire tone of the city, the way people looked and talked and met one another, was Cuban.

— *Joan Didion*, Miami, *1987*

Land of Sunny Shores

> Its climate, sunny, serene, salubrious, seemed like that of Paradise. Though subsequent explorations revealed extensive swamps and widespread barrens, yet there were vast regions of fertility and loveliness, presenting attractions such as can scarcely elsewhere be found upon this globe.
>
> — *John S. C. Abbott, "Florida. Her Crime and Punishment."* Harper's New Monthly Magazine, *November 1866*

Wetlands, Highlands, and Lowlands

Florida's topography can be divided into five basic regions: the coastal lowlands, the central highlands, the Tallahassee hills, the Marianna lowlands, and the western highlands. The flat plains of the coastal lowlands border the Florida coast, rarely rising more than 25 feet (7.6 meters) above sea level. Much of it is swamp and wetlands, including the Everglades at the peninsula's southwestern tip.

The central highlands extend south from the Georgia border down through the center of the state. A region of broad plains and rolling hills, plus freshwater springs and lakes, this area is the center of the state's citrus-growing industry.

Although small compared to the rest of the state, Florida's panhandle encompasses the most topographical variety. Starting west at the Alabama border are the western highlands, mainly a gently sloping plateau criss-crossed by streams. Extending to the Apalachicola River are

DID YOU KNOW?

The majority of Florida's land never rises more than 100 feet (30 m) above sea level. Its highest point, Britton Hill, is 345 feet (105 m) above sea level. That's only 1.6 percent of the height of Alaska's Mt. McKinley, the highest point in the United States.

▼ *From left to right:* St. Petersburg beach; the endangered Florida panther; the Ocala National Forest; the 10,000 Islands; a beach near St. Augustine; Florida pelicans.

the Marianna lowlands, a region with a limestone foundation that is dotted with caves, ponds, and small lakes. To the east are the sand-and-clay Tallahassee hills.

Lakes, Rivers, and Springs

Florida has thirty thousand lakes, most in the central part of the state. The largest is Lake Okeechobee, which covers 680 square miles (1,760 sq km) but has a maximum depth of only 9 feet (2.75 m).

Florida's numerous springs contain mineral waters and are so clear that plant life is visible as far down as 80 feet (24 m) below the surface. The state has seventeen large springs and innumerable smaller ones, located in its central region. Silver Springs, near Ocala, is the largest in Florida. Wakulla Springs, near Tallahassee, is one of the deepest freshwater springs in the world, measuring about 185 feet (56 m) at its deepest point.

Florida's largest river is the St. Johns River, which flows north from Melbourne and runs parallel to the eastern coast before draining into the Atlantic Ocean near Jacksonville. The Apalachicola, in the northwest, not only separates the Marianna lowlands from the Tallahassee hills but also divides the central time zone from the eastern time zone.

Climate

Florida's climate is perhaps its most attractive and distinguishing feature. The weather in the Sunshine State is warm all year, with the peninsula's southern tip sharing the tropical climate of Central America and South America. The rest of the state is considered subtropical. Although it can get unbearably hot and humid in the summer, with temperatures regularly reaching above 90°Fahrenheit (32°Celsius), ocean breezes help keep the coastal areas cooler and more pleasant. Hurricane season lasts from July to October. On average, the state experiences one hurricane each year.

FLORIDA GEOGRAPHY

ATLANTIC OCEAN

Cumberland Island NS

Timucuan Ecological and Historic Preserve

Gulf Islands NS

Chactawhatchee R.

L. Seminole

L. Talquin

Dead L.

St. Joseph Bay

Apalachee Bay

Aucilla R.

Suwannee R.

Sante Fe

St. Johns R.

Newnans L.

Orange L.

Crescent L.

L. George

L. Rousseau

Waccasassa Bay

L. Harris

L. Monroe

L. Apopka

Canaveral NS

GULF OF MEXICO

L. Tohopekaliga

L. Kissimmee

Tampa Bay

Peace R.

Kissimmee R.

L. Istokpoga

L. Okeechobee

Charlotte Harbor

Caloosahachee R.

Big Cypress National Preserve

Biscayne NP

Ponce de León Bay

Florida Bay

Everglades NP

Florida Keys

SCALE/KEY

0   100 Miles

0   100 Kilometers

NP   National Park

NS   National Seashore

▲   Highest Point

   Mountains

In the winter Florida remains relatively mild and can get as warm as 75°F (25°C). North of Miami the temperature may occasionally drop below freezing (possibly damaging crops) but usually only for short periods of time.

Plants and Animals

In Florida consider the flamingo,
Its color passion but its neck a question.
— Robert Penn Warren

About half of Florida is covered by forests, consisting of more than three hundred species of trees. The most common is pine, but other types include ash, beech, cedar, cypress, magnolia, mangrove, and oak; tropical trees such as the palm are found in the southern part of the state.

Major Rivers

Suwannee River
213 miles (343 km) long

St. Johns River
200 miles (322 km) long

Choctawatche
180 miles (290 km) long

DID YOU KNOW?

Okeechobee comes from a Seminole word meaning "big water."

Florida features a diverse animal life, with more than one hundred mammal species and four hundred bird species. Urban development, logging, and other factors threaten many species with extinction. Panthers, crocodiles, and manatees are among those Florida animals officially designated as endangered species.

The bird population in Florida has the largest colonies of anhingas, egrets, herons, ibises, and pelicans north of the Caribbean. Many of these marsh birds live in the Everglades. Land birds include eagles, hawks, owls, and quails; coastal birds include flamingos, gulls, sandpipers, ospreys, and cormorants.

Florida boasts the greatest variety of fish in the world. Freshwater lakes and rivers contain bass, bream, catfish, and crappies; ocean fish are bluefish, groupers, mackerel, marlins, red snapper, sea trout, and tarpon, as well as shellfish such as clams, crabs, crayfish, oysters, scallops, and shrimp. Marine mammals include dolphins, porpoises, and manatees.

The Everglades

There are no other Everglades in the world. They are, they have always been, one of the unique regions of the earth, remote, never wholly known.
— Marjory Stoneman Douglas

The Everglades, at Florida's southern tip, is a vast area of swampy grasslands fed by the Kissimmee River and Lake Okeechobee. Before Florida's land boom these wetlands covered almost 11,000 square miles (28,490 sq km) and sustained all kinds of wildlife. Today, because of extensive draining and an ever-growing population, half of the original wetlands have been drained and covered with landfill.

To help preserve the region, President Harry S. Truman established Everglades National Park in 1947. The park, which draws over one million visitors every year, is an important breeding ground for tropical wading birds such as the great blue heron. Over time the drainage of water from the land — conducted partly to protect the area but also to encourage farming and urban development and to supply fresh water to the surrounding region — has upset the delicate balance of the Everglades's ecosystem. Researchers and conservationists are studying ways to reverse this problem and protect the many plant and animal species that live in the Everglades.

DID YOU KNOW?

Florida's coastline — measuring 1,350 miles (2,173 km), not counting lagoons, bays, and barrier islands — is the second longest of any state after Alaska.

Michigan, however, has a longer freshwater shoreline, consisting of more than 3,200 miles (5,150 km).

Florida's Mermaids

The West Indian manatee, or sea cow resembles a walrus but is actually related to the elephant. The mermaid myth may have arisen when sailors mistook manatees, with their armlike flippers and fishlike tails, for humans sitting on the rocks.

The Florida Manatee Sanctuary Act of 1978 makes it a crime for anyone to harm or disturb one of the animals. Currently there are about three thousand West Indian manatees left in the United States, most in Florida.

DID YOU KNOW?

Among Florida's native reptiles are turtles, tortoises, lizards, frogs, and forty species of snakes — including the poisonous coral, rattlesnake, moccasin, and copperhead.

Sunshine Gold

> Like many wildly successful Floridians, Francis X. Kingsbury was a transplant. He had moved to the Sunshine State in balding middle age, alone and uprooted, never expecting that he would become a multimillionaire.
>
> — *Carl Hiaasen,* Native Tongue

Florida's economy, one of the fastest growing in the country, owes much to its climate — and to the millions of tourists eager to enjoy it every year. Amusement parks such as Walt Disney World and Universal Studios in Orlando and world-class beaches in Miami and Daytona bring in billions of tourist dollars annually. Golf, hunting, fishing, and national parks such as the Everglades are other popular attractions that help make tourism the largest income-producing activity in the state.

The service industry accounts for more than 30 percent of all of Florida's jobs and contributes the most to Florida's gross state product. This includes employees of theme parks and hotels as well as those who work in fields such as law and medicine. Florida's economy also depends on those who come to stay. Many people move to Florida for their "golden" years. Real estate, insurance, and finance are areas of the service industry that have benefited from Florida's prosperous retirement communities.

Big Fish in a Big Pond

Fishing is a major source of commercial income, with an annual catch worth $215 million. Two-thirds of that comes from shrimp, lobsters, groupers, and clams. Florida contributes 10 percent of the U.S. shrimp catch every year, largely from shrimp grounds off Key West. Florida also supplies the national market with such freshwater and saltwater fish as catfish, mackerel, marlin, swordfish, and tuna.

DID YOU KNOW?

There is no word in the English language that rhymes with "orange."

Top Employers
(of workers age sixteen and over)

Wholesale and retail trade 2,295,385	. . . .	38%
Services 1,828,452	. . . .	31%
Government workers 833,144	. . . .	14%
Manufacturing 608,821	. . . .	10%
Finance, insurance, and real estate 468,324	. . . .	8%

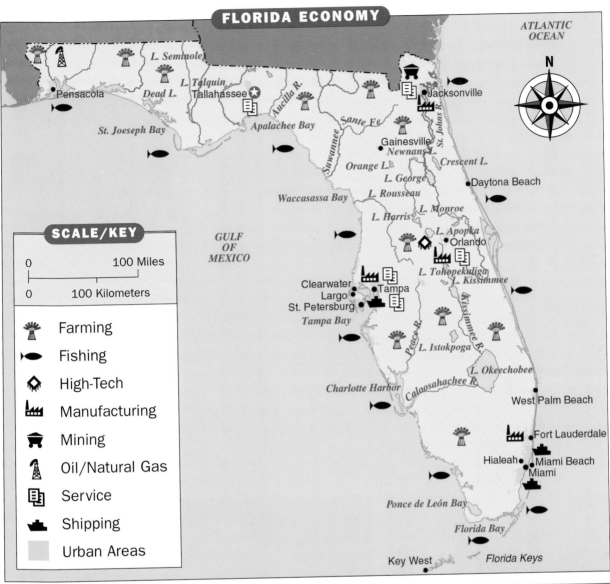

FLORIDA ECONOMY

ATLANTIC OCEAN

GULF OF MEXICO

SCALE/KEY

0 — 100 Miles

0 — 100 Kilometers

- 🌾 Farming
- 🐟 Fishing
- ◈ High-Tech
- 🏭 Manufacturing
- ⛏ Mining
- Oil/Natural Gas
- 🗐 Service
- Shipping
- Urban Areas

Pensacola, L. Seminole, Dead L., L. Talquin, Tallahassee, St. Joeseph Bay, Apalachee Bay, Suwannee, Sante Fe, Aucilla R., Jacksonville, Gainesville, Newnans L., Orange L., L. George, L. Rousseau, Crescent L., Daytona Beach, Waccasassa Bay, L. Harris, L. Monroe, L. Apopka, Orlando, L. Tohopekaliga, L. Kissimmee, Clearwater, Largo, St. Petersburg, Tampa, Tampa Bay, Peace R., L. Istokpoga, Kissimmee R., L. Okeechobee, Caloosahachee R., Charlotte Harbor, West Palm Beach, Fort Lauderdale, Hialeah, Miami Beach, Miami, Ponce de León Bay, Florida Bay, Key West, Florida Keys, St. Johns R.

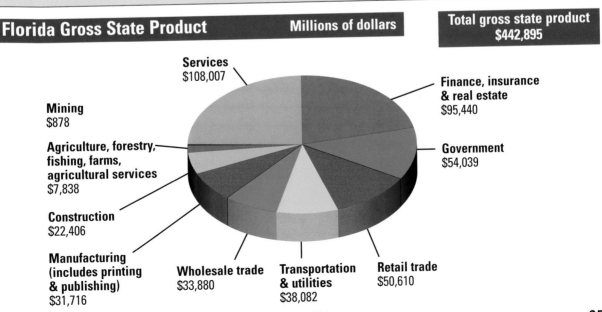

Florida Gross State Product — Millions of dollars

Total gross state product $442,895

- Services $108,007
- Finance, insurance & real estate $95,440
- Government $54,039
- Retail trade $50,610
- Transportation & utilities $38,082
- Wholesale trade $33,880
- Manufacturing (includes printing & publishing) $31,716
- Construction $22,406
- Agriculture, forestry, fishing, farms, agricultural services $7,838
- Mining $878

Source: U.S. Department of Commerce, Bureau of Economic Analysis, Regional Economic Analysis Division.

Down on the Farm

An orange grown in Florida usually has a thin and tightly fitting skin, and it is also heavy with juice. Californians say that if you want to eat a Florida orange you have to get into a bathtub first. . . . In Florida, it is said that you can run over a California orange with a ten-ton truck and not even wet the pavement.
— John McPhee, *Oranges* (1967)

The first citrus trees were introduced to Florida near St. Augustine in the late 1500s; today three-quarters of the orange and grapefruit crops in the United States come from Florida and are grown mostly in the south-central region, between Orlando and Okeechobee. Groves of limes, tangerines, tangelos, and temples also flourish in the subtropical climate. The citrus is processed into various food products — fresh orange juice, canned and frozen juice, and canned fruit sections — which adds significantly to the income from Florida's manufacturing industry. Florida also grows exotic fruits such as guavas, kumquats, loquats, and papayas, as well as more common fruits such as bananas, grapes, peaches, strawberries, and watermelons.

Tomatoes, grown in the southern part of the state, are Florida's second-largest crop. Vegetables include beans,

▼ *From left to right:* The *Apollo 11* spacecraft launches on July 16, 1969; the Walt Disney World staff gathers for a photo.

sweet corn, potatoes, and squash. Field crops produced are tobacco, peanuts, hay, cotton, and sugarcane. Florida leads the country in sugarcane production, growing 40 percent of the nation's total. Twenty percent of Florida's farm income comes from livestock and related products such as cattle, poultry, milk, and eggs. Florida is also renowned for breeding top-quality thoroughbred horses, mostly near Ocala.

Treasures from the Earth

The excitement spread with the rumor of immense profits. The owners of low lands along the river, who had been giving them to anyone who would pay their taxes, now dreamed of millions.
— An eyewitness to the phosphate boom, Peace River Valley, late nineteenth century.

Florida is rich in phosphate, a mineral used primarily to make fertilizer (and to a much lesser extent, animal feed and laundry detergent). Seventy-five percent of the nation's phosphate and 25 percent of the world supply come from Florida, where the mineral is extracted from mines in the west-central region. Along with Georgia, Florida has one of the largest deposits of fuller's earth. This clay's surface attracts oil and grease, and while it is used industrially by factory workers to clean up oil spills, it is also sold to consumers as the main ingredient in kitty litter.

The Tech Industry

After food production the most profitable area of Florida's manufacturing industry is in the electrical and electronics sector. Florida has kept pace with the modern technology boom, ranking fifth in the nation's employers of high-tech jobs. More than 180,000 Floridians work developing or producing software, telecommunications equipment, broadcasting devices, Internet applications, and semiconductors and other electrical components.

Florida also has a major presence in the nation's aeronautical industry, thanks to Cape Canaveral's space program. The Mercury and Apollo missions were launched here, as were the first U.S. satellite and the various space shuttle missions.

How to Sell the Most Orange Juice? Concentrate.

Florida wouldn't be the world's second-largest seller of orange juice if not for the efforts of Cedric Donald "C.D." Atkins, Louis Gardner MacDowell, and Edwin L. Moore. During World War II the U.S. government asked the Florida Citrus Commission to create an orange juice product that could be transported to troops fighting in Europe. Atkins, MacDowell, and Moore were charged with the task, and they tinkered for three years before perfecting an economical method of chilling, canning, and then freezing the beverage. By the time a patent was issued, the war was over, but their frozen orange juice was already being used commercially.

Presidential Jackpot

> Florida is a big tamale. It's not only a hot tamale, it's the only tamale that counts up here now — twenty-five electoral votes. He who wins Florida wins it all.
>
> — *CBS anchorman Dan Rather, presidential election night, 2000*

F lorida has had six constitutions dating from 1838, 1861, 1865, 1868, 1885, and 1968. The first, written in 1838 under Florida's territorial government, was the state's governing document until Florida seceded from the Union.

Florida's 1865 constitution, drawn up to qualify for readmittance into the Union, was rejected by Congress because it did not give freed slaves the right to vote. Florida was placed under federal military rule for the next three years but gained admittance with its 1868 Reconstruction Constitution, which extended voting rights to African Americans. The 1885 constitution established Florida's basic government and remained in place until the current constitution was drafted and ratified in the 1968 general election.

Executive Branch

Rather like the president and vice president, Florida's governor and lieutenant governor are elected as a team, serving terms of four years. State term limits dictate that a governor cannot be reelected after serving two terms in a row. The governor also has a six-member cabinet made up of the secretary of state, attorney general, comptroller, treasurer and commissioner of insurance, commissioner of agriculture, and commissioner of education. Florida's cabinet is unique. It is the only state cabinet made up of six independently elected officials that do not have to answer to the governor; they stand on equal footing with the governor.

The Constitution

We, the people of the State of Florida, being grateful to Almighty God for our constitutional liberty, in order to secure its benefits, perfect our government, insure domestic tranquility, maintain public order, and guarantee equal civil and political rights to all, do ordain and establish this constitution.

Preamble to Florida's current constitution

Elected Posts in the Executive Branch		
Office	Length of Term	Term Limits
Governor and Lieutenant Governor	4 years	2 terms in a 12-year period
Attorney General	4 years	2 terms in a 12-year period
Chief Financial Officer	4 years	2 terms in a 12-year period
Agricultural Commissioner	4 years	2 terms in a 12-year period

The Legislative Branch

Florida's legislature consists of a Senate and House of Representatives. The state legislature meets every year for a single sixty-day session, which traditionally opens on the first Tuesday in March. Special sessions may be convened by the governor, by joint agreement of the leaders of each house, or by a three-fifths vote of all House and Senate members.

To ensure equal representation based on population, the state's constitution requires reapportionment (redivision of legislative districts) every ten years or after every federal census. This issue first arose in 1965, when a federal court ordered Florida to reapportion and then, after rejecting Florida's proposed plan, drafted its own reapportionment plan.

▼ The old Florida state capitol building (foreground) is today a state museum. Behind the original building rises the new capitol complex, completed in 1977.

The Judicial Branch

The bench of Florida's Supreme Court seats seven justices, each appointed by the governor to a six-year term. Every year the seven justices elect a new chief justice. The governor appoints the judges for the state's five district courts of appeals to six-year terms, while Florida's voters elect the judges for the twenty circuit courts and sixty-seven county courts.

▲ The Florida legislature in session.

County Government

Florida is divided into sixty-seven counties, each of which may draw up its own special charter if approved by the state legislature and the county residents. Most counties are governed by a board of five commissioners, elected from each of five districts to four-year terms. County voters also elect the county sheriff, election supervisor, and tax collector, among other positions.

Chartered counties may make their own laws, provided those laws do not conflict with the Florida State Constitution. This form of self-governance is known as "home rule," which the Florida Association of Counties defines as "the right of the people to determine and implement a public purpose at the grassroots level." Such counties may also join together to create consolidated governments.

State Revenues

Sixty percent of the government's revenue comes from taxes, including a 6 percent sales and use tax, a corporate income tax, and an estate tax. Unlike most states, however, Florida does not have a personal income tax. The remaining 40 percent of the state's revenue comes from federal grants and other government programs.

Legislature			
House	**Number of Members**	**Length of Term**	**Term Limits**
Senate	40 senators	4 years	No more than 2 consecutive terms
House of Representatives	120 representatives	2 years	No more than 2 consecutive terms

Florida and National Politics

So for me this campaign ends . . . with gratitude to our truly tireless campaign staff and volunteers, including all those who worked so hard in Florida for the last 36 days.
— Presidential candidate Al Gore, concession speech on December 13, 2000

Historically Florida has elected Democratic politicians to state and federal office, but that appears to be changing. From 1880 to 1948 the Democratic candidates for president lost in Florida only once, in 1928. (Herbert Hoover was the Republican candidate that year, beating Alfred Smith in a landslide.) Florida's voters also tended to put Democratic candidates in the U.S. Congress, and the state legislature had more Democrats than Republicans. In the last few decades, however, Florida has elected Republican governors and voted for Republican presidential candidates. In 2001 the state legislature had many more Republicans than Democrats, and the majority of Florida's U.S. representatives were Republican.

Florida became the focus of intense political scrutiny during the 2000 presidential election, which was the closest in history. On election night television networks —using exit polls to make educated guesses at each state's results — first declared Democratic candidate Al Gore the winner in the critical Florida vote, then Republican candidate George W. Bush. Immediately after Gore called Bush to congratulate him on his presidential victory, however, the networks determined that the race was too close to call. Because Florida's twenty-five electoral votes would tip the contest one way or the other, disputed ballots in several Florida counties were studied and recounted, and the outcome of the presidential election remained in limbo for over a month. With thousands of voters claiming that their votes had not been properly counted, Florida became a national symbol for the need for electoral reform. After a controversial Supreme Court decision effectively ended the recount, the official tally showed Bush to have 1,725 more votes in Florida than Gore. The state's electoral votes were certified for Bush, who subsequently assumed the presidency.

▼ A contested "butterfly" ballot in the Florida election. It was argued that the people had difficulty lining the names up with the correct punch hole. The list of presidential candidates also took up several pages, and some voters were instructed to punch a hole on every page. Some voters ended up voting for more than one presidential candidate, which caused their votes to be disqualified.

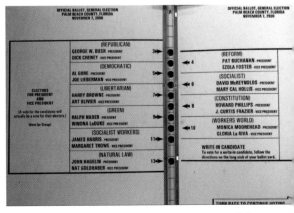

The Happiest Place on Earth

Disney World has acquired by now something of the air of a national shrine. American parents who don't take their children there sense obscurely that they have failed in some fundamental way, like Muslims who never made it to Mecca.
— *Simon Hoggart*, America: A User's Guide

To some visitors, Florida would not be Florida without Walt Disney World. This dream vacation destination is a real-life success story, one that has had a significant impact on the local economy. Disney World, the largest tourist attraction in the United States, consists of four parks in Orlando's Disney complex. The most popular of the four parks, the Magic Kingdom, draws over fifteen million people every year. It opened in 1971, modeled after Walt Disney's first theme park, Disneyland's Magic Kingdom in Anaheim, California.

Epcot, Disney World's second most popular attraction, is an acronym for Experimental Prototype Community of Tomorrow. A combination of world's fair and science

◀ The Walt Disney World monorail, with Epcot in the distance.

DID YOU KNOW?

The Walt Disney World complex stretches over 43 square miles (111 sq km), an area twice the size of New York's Manhattan Island.

museum, the park provides a hands-on look at different aspects of technology, the sciences, history, and international culture. The park's centerpiece structure is Spaceship Earth, a seventeen-story geodesic dome visible from miles away.

Of the two other parks at Walt Disney World, Disney-MGM Studios offers rides and shows based on popular Disney films, gives behind-the-scene tours of animation and live-action films, and also serves as a working film and movie studio. Disney's Animal Kingdom, the newest addition, is a 500-acre (200-ha) park featuring live animals and rides and shows.

▲ A building in South Beach, the art deco district of Miami Beach.

Fun in the Sun

No point in Florida is more than 60 miles (96 kilometers) from the sea, a fact that appeals to both residents and vacationers. One thousand miles (1,609 km) of Florida's sandy coastline contain some of the world's most famous beaches. The sand on Florida's west coast beaches is soft and dazzlingly white because of its high concentration of quartz. Ocean breezes keep temperatures relatively cool in the summer months, ensuring that beach season in Florida lasts all year long.

Every spring, college students from around the country head to Florida for their weeklong spring break vacations. Traditionally Fort Lauderdale in southern Florida and Daytona Beach in central Florida have been the destinations of choice, but in recent years Panama City Beach (on the Panhandle, near Tallahassee) has grown in popularity.

When Cubans fled Fidel Castro's revolutionary regime in the 1960s, they congregated in a neighborhood west of downtown Miami. The area, known as Little Havana, is now a melting pot of Latin American culture that also includes ethnic groups from El Salvador, Nicaragua, Guatemala, and the Dominican Republic. It is a neighborhood of traditional Cuban bungalows, street

DID YOU KNOW?
South Beach has the largest concentration of Art Deco buildings in the world — eight hundred buildings on Ocean Drive are designed in Streamline Moderne, a Floridian variation of the classic style.

vendors, and cigar factories. English is rarely spoken, Latin music of every variety can be heard everywhere, and authentic Cuban and other Latin American cuisines are readily available.

Miami Beach, a barrier island 2 miles (3 km) off the mainland, is famous for the striking art deco architecture at its southern tip, a hip area known as South Beach. These fantastic structures provide an appropriate backdrop to the stylish models, actors, and other celebrities who frequent South Beach's nightlife scene.

Colleges and Universities

Of Florida's eleven public universities, the University of Florida in Gainesville is the oldest (founded as East Florida Seminary in 1853) and largest. With more than forty-three thousand students, it is the sixth largest university in the country. Florida State University also began as a seminary school, going through various transitions before assuming its current name and status in 1947. Students number about thirty-five thousand.

▼ Sun and surf at the Florida Keys.

▲ The Miami Dolphins at play.

The Sporting Life

Baseball comes to life each season in Florida, where twenty major-league teams engage in spring training. They also play exhibition games in the so-called Grapefruit League, a

Sport	Team	Home
Baseball	Florida Marlins	Pro Player Stadium, Miami
	Tampa Bay Devil Rays	Tropicana Field, St. Petersburg
Basketball	Miami Heat	AmericanAirlines Arena, Miami
	Orlando Magic	TD Waterhouse Centre, Orlando
Women's Basketball	Miami Sol (WNBA)	AmericanAirlines Arena, Miami
	Orlando Miracle (WNBA)	TD Waterhouse Centre, Orlando
Football	Tampa Bay Buccaneers	Raymond James Stadium, Tampa Bay
	Miami Dolphins	Pro Player Stadium, Miami
	Jacksonville Jaguars	Alltel Stadium, Jacksonville
Hockey	Florida Panthers	National Car Rental Center, Sunrise
	Tampa Bay Lightning	Ice Palace Arena, Tampa Bay
Soccer	Tampa Bay Mutiny	Raymond James Stadium, Tampa Bay
	Miami Fusion	Lockhart Stadium, Ft. Lauderdale

State Greats

Football is huge in Florida, from its many bowl games, to its intrastate college rivalries, to its three NFL teams — the Miami Dolphins, Tampa Bay Buccaneers, and Jacksonville Jaguars. The oldest of these three teams, the Miami Dolphins, is arguably one of the most recognized sports franchises in the United States. Its Hall of Famers include Dan Marino (quarterback from 1983–1999) and coach Don Shula (head coach from 1970–1995). The team has played in five Super Bowls, winning twice — in 1973 and 1974. Upon entry into the American Football League in 1965, the Dolphins decided on their team name based on a contest. Among the 19,843 entries, more than one thousand different names were suggested. More than 620 entrants, however, suggested "Dolphins."

popular attraction for fans because ticket prices are less expensive than for regular season games.

Florida plays host to five college bowl games: the Orange, Gator, Citrus, Blockbuster, and Hall of Fame Bowls. Two of the state's public universities, the University of Florida and Florida State University, have maintained a fierce football rivalry in recent years.

National Parks

Of Florida's three national parks, Everglades National Park — 1.5 million acres (607,050 sq km) of wetlands — is the crown jewel, the largest subtropical wilderness in the United States and sanctuary to a multitude of rare, endangered, and exotic animals. Dry Tortugas National Park, a cluster of islands 70 miles (113 km) west of Key

Art Deco: Marrying the Old and the New

The original art deco style grew out of the 1925 Exposition Internationale des Arts Décoratifs et Industriels Modernes in Paris, an exhibit combining various artistic trends — such as the geometric patterns of cubism and the Egyptian themes of art nouveau — with a modern, technological approach. On Ocean Drive in Miami Beach, hotels and other buildings feature streamlined shapes; images of flamingos, sunbursts, and tropical motifs; bright colors; neon; and vertical lines.

▼ Alligators in the Everglades.

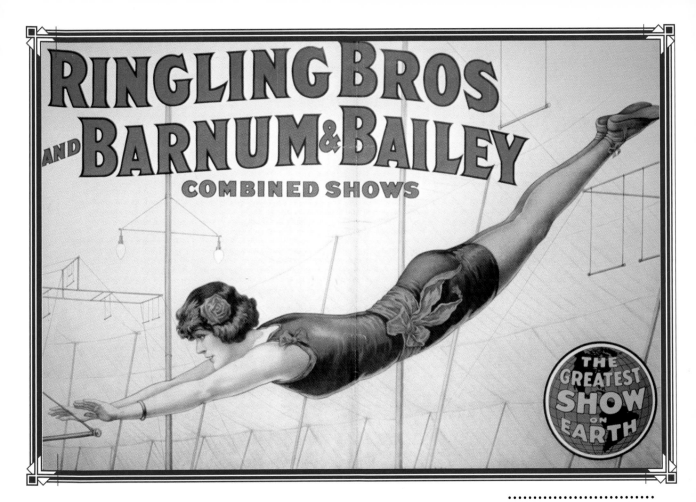

RINGLING BROS AND BARNUM & BAILEY COMBINED SHOWS

THE GREATEST SHOW ON EARTH

▲ A vintage poster for the Ringling Bros. and Barnum & Bailey Circus.

West reachable only by boat or seaplane, is known for its sea turtles, other marine and bird life, and coral reefs. Biscayne National Park, near Miami, also contains a spectacular coral reef as well as a large mangrove forest.

Museums

The John and Mable Ringling Museum of Art in Sarasota, affiliated with Florida State University, is the largest university/museum complex in the United States. It features a museum of European and American art, the Ringling mansion, and the Ringling Museum of the Circus, which traces the history of the circus that began as a wagon show in 1870 and grew into today's famed Ringling Bros. and Barnum & Bailey, "The Greatest Show on Earth." John Ringling, one of the original brothers, moved the circus's winter quarters to Sarasota in 1927.

Florida's many other museums include the Museum of Florida History in Tallahassee, the Florida Museum of Natural History in Gainesville, and the Henry Morrison Flagler Museum in Palm Beach.

Famous Floridians

Sing a song full of the faith that the dark past has taught us.
Sing a song full of the hope that the present has brought us.
Facing the rising sun of our new day begun,
Let us march on 'til victory is won.

— *Excerpt from "Lift Ev'ry Voice and Sing,"*
lyrics by James Weldon Johnson

Following are only a few of the thousands of people who lived, died, or spent most of their lives in Florida and made extraordinary contributions to the state and the nation.

OSCEOLA
SEMINOLE LEADER

BORN: *circa 1804, Georgia*
DIED: *January 30, 1838, Charleston, SC*

Osceola is considered to be one of the great Seminole leaders. He was born to a Creek mother in 1804, and the tribe relocated to Florida after the Creek War of 1813 to 1814. A skilled orator, Osceola was a leading voice for Seminole resistance after the Indian Removal Act was passed in 1830. During the Second Seminole War, Osceola earned a reputation as a fierce fighter. In October 1837 Osceola went to a meeting with U.S. troops, believing they were going to discuss terms of a truce. Instead, they captured Osceola and put him in prison. He died the next year from a throat infection caused by malaria. His gravestone reads "Patriot and Warrior."

JAMES WELDON JOHNSON
POET AND DIPLOMAT

BORN: *June 17, 1871, Jacksonville*
DIED: *June 26, 1938, Wiscasset, ME*

In 1900 James Johnson, a high school principal in Jacksonville, collaborated with his brother John on a song celebrating Abraham Lincoln's birthday. "Lift Ev'ry Voice and Sing" (based on Johnson's poem of the same name) eventually became known as the "Negro National Anthem." Johnson also anonymously published a novel, *Autobiography of an Ex-Colored Man* in 1912. It received little attention, faring much better when reissued under his own name in 1927. Johnson, also the first African American to be admitted to the Florida bar, held diplomatic posts in Venezuela and Nicaragua, headed the National Association for the Advancement of Colored People (NAACP) in the 1920s, and taught creative literature at Fisk University.

MARY MCLEOD BETHUNE

EDUCATOR

BORN: *July 10, 1875, Mayesville, SC*
DIED: *May 18, 1955, Daytona Beach*

The daughter of former slaves, Mary McLeod Bethune was the first African-American woman to establish a school in the United States that became a four-year accredited college. In 1904 she opened the Daytona Educational and Industrial Training School for Negro Girls on the site of a former Daytona Beach city dump. By 1923 the school had become co-ed and was renamed the Bethune-Cookman College. It had six hundred students and thirty-two faculty members. An adviser to five U.S. presidents, Bethune was known to respond to people who condescendingly called her "auntie" by asking, "Which one of my sister's children are you?"

A. PHILIP RANDOLPH

LABOR LEADER

BORN: *April 15, 1889, Crescent City*
DIED: *May 16, 1979, New York, NY*

Asa Philip Randolph rose to prominence as a labor organizer when porters for the powerful Pullman Company asked him to help them form a union. Randolph launched the Brotherhood of Sleeping Car Porters

in 1925 and spent more than ten years fighting with the Pullman Company to negotiate better working conditions. Perhaps Randolph's most famous achievement was his march on Washington on August 28, 1963, which he organized as vice president of the AFL–CIO. The country was in the midst of a tough economic recession that was disproportionately affecting blacks. More than 250,000 people marched peacefully from the Washington Monument to the Lincoln Memorial, singing songs and waving signs. The Civil Rights Act of 1964 was signed the following year.

ZORA NEALE HURSTON

WRITER

BORN: *January 7, 1903, Eatonville*
DIED: *January 28, 1960, Fort Pierce*

In writing about the black culture of the rural South, Hurston refused to portray her characters as victims. At age sixteen, Hurston worked as a wardrobe girl in a traveling Gilbert and Sullivan theatrical company. This brought her to New York during the Harlem Renaissance. She studied anthropology at Barnard and Vodun culture in Haiti before beginning her writing career. Her second and most celebrated novel, *Their Eyes Were Watching God*, was published in 1937. One of the first African-American writers to integrate folk traditions into modern literature, Hurston was a major influence on African-American writers such as Ralph Ellison and Toni Morrison. Hurston died in obscurity — her grave remained unmarked until novelist Alice Walker placed a tombstone on it in 1973.

"RED" BARBER

SPORTS BROADCASTER

BORN: *February 17, 1908, Columbus, MS*
DIED: *October 22, 1992, Tallahassee*

Walter Larier Barber was famous for his colorful style of calling baseball games, describing a player as "tearing up the pea patch" or "sitting in the catbird seat" or "running like a bunny with his tail on fire." His first radio job was at the University of Florida's station WRUF. After broadcasting with the Cincinnati Reds (a job he auditioned for during spring training), he went to work for the Brooklyn Dodgers in 1939. For games away from home, Barber recreated the action that was relayed to him by teletype. On August 26, 1939, Barber broadcast the first televised professional baseball game — a doubleheader between the Dodgers and (coincidentally) the Reds. After a contractual dispute with Dodger management in 1953, Barber went across town to broadcast games for the New York Yankees and stayed there until 1966. "Baseball is dull only to dull minds," he once said.

JACQUELINE COCHRAN

PILOT

BORN: *circa 1910, Pensacola*
DIED: *August 9, 1980, Indio, CA*

Jacqueline Cochran was the first woman to fly faster than the speed of sound. Born to a poor family, she trained as a beautician. In 1932 she took her first flying lesson and began racing competitively in the late 1930s and early 1940s. On May 18, 1963, Cochran broke the sound barrier in an F-86 Sabre, traveling at 625.5 miles (1,007 km) per hour. She broke many other barriers in the course of her flying career. She was the first woman to make a blind landing; the first woman to fly a warplane across the Atlantic Ocean; and the first woman civilian to be awarded the Distinguished Service Medal (for her work training female pilots in World War II). By 1961 Cochran held more speed records than any other pilot — male or female — in the world.

"CANNONBALL" ADDERLEY

JAZZ MUSICIAN

BORN: *September 15, 1928, Tampa*
DIED: *August 8, 1975, Gary, IN*

Born Julian Edwin Adderley ("Cannonball" came from "Cannibal," a childhood nickname he earned due to his large appetite), this alto saxophonist was a high school band director in Fort Lauderdale. One day during a 1955 visit to New York, he joined in on a performance at the Café Bohemia — and caused such a stir that he moved to New York to play jazz full time. The quintet Adderley formed with his younger brother, Nat, broke up in 1957, but Adderley's next collaboration hit gold. Along with tenor saxophonist John Coltrane, he joined trumpeter Miles Davis's sextet and participated in such classics as the 1959 album *Kind of Blue*. With his brother, Adderley formed a second quintet and recorded several successful albums until his death from a stroke.

JORGE MAS CANOSA

POLITICAL ACTIVIST

BORN: *September 21, 1939, Santiago de Cuba*
DIED: *November 23, 1997, Miami*

Jorge Mas Canosa was exiled from Cuba at an early age after protesting the Communist regime. As a poor immigrant in Miami, he worked at various low-paying jobs (including one as a milkman) before buying a small telecommunications company and turning it into a vast empire. Mas Canosa's greatest accomplishments, however, were in the political arena. In 1981 he founded a powerful lobbying group, the Cuban American National Foundation (CANF), serving as its chairman until his death. Perhaps the most influential Cuban American in the United States, Mas Canosa never wavered in his passionate prodemocracy, anti-Communist message and in his attempts to overthrow Castro.

JIM MORRISON

ROCK MUSICIAN

BORN: *December 8, 1943, Melbourne*
DIED: *July 3, 1971, Paris, France*

The charismatic lead singer for the rock band the Doors, Morrison came to

symbolize the rebellious 1960s for both his critics and his fans. Morrison and his University of California (UCLA) film-school classmate Ray Manzarek formed the Doors in 1965. With its dark, experimental, and richly layered songs, the band became hugely popular and critically acclaimed overnight; the handsome Morrison, who sang, wrote, and performed with brooding intensity, became a rock idol. Morrison's wild behavior sometimes attracted more attention than his music; in 1969 he was arrested for indecent exposure during a concert in Miami. His grave in Poets' Corner at Pere Lachaise Cemetery in France has became a rock shrine of sorts, attracting scores of fans every year.

JANET RENO

U.S. ATTORNEY GENERAL

BORN: *July 21, 1938, Miami*

Janet Reno became the first woman U.S. attorney general when President Bill Clinton appointed her in 1993. Before that, Reno (whose Danish-immigrant father reportedly changed his last name from Rasmussen to Reno after looking at a map of Nevada) served as state attorney for Florida's Dade County for fifteen years. As attorney general, Reno gained a reputation for being independent, and her tenure was often marked by controversy. She offered to resign, for example, after she sent FBI agents to raid the Branch Davidian religious cult in Waco, Texas, and eighty people died in the ensuing fire. Reno served for eight years, the longest term of any attorney general in U.S. history.

Florida
History At-A-Glance

1513
Juan Ponce de León lands near present-day St. Augustine, claims the land for Spain, and names it Florida.

1528
Panfilo de Narváez leads an expedition to Florida.

1539
Hernando de Soto leads an expedition through Florida.

1564
French Huguenots build Fort Caroline on the St. Johns River.

1565
Pedro Menéndez, sent by King Philip II of Spain, captures Fort Caroline and founds St. Augustine.

1586
Sir Francis Drake loots and burns St. Augustine.

1763
Spain cedes Florida to Britain in return for Havana, Cuba, at the end of the Seven Years' War. Florida is divided into East and West Florida.

1783
Britain gives Florida back to Spain at the end of the Revolutionary War.

1821
The United States officially gains control of Florida in the Adams-Onis Treaty.

1822
Congress organizes the Territory of Florida.

1835–42
The Second Seminole War drives most of the Seminole Indians from Florida.

1600   **1700**   **1800**

1492
Christopher Columbus comes to the New World.

1607
Capt. John Smith and three ships land on Virginia coast and start first English settlement in New World — Jamestown.

1754–63
French and Indian War.

1773
Boston Tea Party.

1776
Declaration of Independence adopted July 4.

1777
Articles of Confederation adopted by Continental Congress.

1787
U.S. Constitution written.

1812–14
War of 1812.

United States
History At-A-Glance

1845
Florida is admitted to the Union as the twenty-seventh state.

1861
Florida secedes from the Union and joins the Confederacy.

1864
Confederate troops triumph over Union forces at the Battle of Olustee.

1868
Florida is readmitted to the Union.

1920–25
Florida's population increases dramatically as the state experiences a boom in land development.

1939–45
Thousands of U.S. troops train in Florida for World War II.

1958
Explorer I, the first U.S. satellite, is launched from Cape Canaveral.

1963
Cape Canaveral is renamed Cape Kennedy in honor of President John F. Kennedy. (The name was changed back in 1973.)

1969
Florida's present constitution is adopted.

1971
Walt Disney World opens on October 1.

1992
Hurricane Andrew strikes the southern Florida coast, killing forty people and causing over $20 billion in damage.

2000
Controversy over Florida's election results delays the outcome of the presidential election for over a month.

1800	1900	2000

1848
Gold discovered in California draws eighty thousand prospectors in the 1849 Gold Rush.

1861–65
Civil War.

1869
Transcontinental Railroad is completed.

1917–1918
U.S. involvement in World War I.

1929
Stock market crash ushers in Great Depression.

1941–45
U.S. involvement in World War II.

1950–53
U.S. fights in the Korean War.

1964–73
U.S. involvement in Vietnam War.

2000
George W. Bush wins the closest presidential election in history.

2001
A terrorist attack in which four hijacked airliners crash into New York City's World Trade Center, the Pentagon, and farmland in western Pennsylvania leaves thousands dead or injured.

▼ Silver Springs circa 1951.

SCENIC PHOTO SUB 3

Festivals and Fun For All

Check web site for exact date and directions.

Florida Manatee Festival, Crystal River

A three-day event designed to raise awareness about the endangered Florida manatee.

www.loc.gov/bicentennial/propage/FL/fl-5_h_thurman3.html

Florida Folk Festival, White Springs

For nearly fifty years the 850-acre (344-ha) Stephen Foster State Folk Culture Center has come alive with music, dance, and stories.

www.flheritage.com/folkfest

Cathedral Festival, St. Augustine

Four days of entertainment, rides, food, and fun!

www.cathedralfestival.com

Coconut Grove Arts Festival, Coconut Grove

Every year the festival hosts the work of more than 330 artists and artisans from around the world.

coconutgroveartsfest.com

The Clewiston Sugar Festival, Clewiston

Celebrating the sweetness of one of Florida's crops at a sugarcane harvest fest.

members.aol.com/kq4ym/sugfest.html

Disney's Martial Arts Festival, Orlando

Kids and adults compete in martial arts of every discipline.

www.i-can.net/dmaf

Shorebird Festival, Naples

Learn the joys of bird-watching at this celebration of the many birds that visit Florida's shores.

www.floridaconservation.org/viewing/wbs/fffbriggs.htm

Orlando International Fringe Festival, Orlando

The Orlando International Fringe Festival is a ten-day celebration of the theatrical and performing arts held in the streets, theaters, and converted office spaces of downtown Orlando.

www.orlandofringe.com

Florida Citrus Festival, Winter Haven

Held in a 55-foot (17-m) high, 170-foot (52-m) diameter dome painted to look like an orange half, this festival highlights the history and importance of Florida oranges.

citrusfestival.com

Wings and Strings American Music Festival, Polk City

Regional and nationally renowned musicians play Texas swing, "new" grass, Cajun, contra, and traditional bluegrass.

www.wingsandstrings.com

Bach Festival, **Winter Park**
The Bach Festival Choir and Orchestra join forces with guest soloists in an acoustically and visually ideal setting, performing concerts that have inspired audiences for six decades.
www.bachfestivalflorida.org

Florida Strawberry Festival, **Plant City**
Ripe strawberries, fresh off the vine, are a feature of this annual festival.
www.flstrawberryfestival.com

LYNX Jazz Festival, **Orlando**
A free three-day event filled with the sounds of blues, gospel, Dixieland, Latin, horns, and big band acts.
www.jazzorlando.com

International Festival, **Daytona Beach**
Featuring the London Symphony Orchestra on the Florida shores, audiences may relax and soak up the sun at this festival of beautiful music and entertainment from around the world.
www.fif-lso.org

◄ Carnaval in Miami is the largest Hispanic festival in the nation. This two-week event includes street parties, music festivals, cooking contests, a beauty pageant, and sporting events — all intended to share the bounties of Hispanic culture with the rest of the world.

Books

Andryszewski, Tricia. *Marjory Stoneman Douglas: Friend of the Everglades*. Brookfield, CT: Millbrook Press, 1994. Naturalist Marjory Stoneman Douglas battled for nearly seventy-five years to preserve the Florida Everglades. This is her story.

Blaustein, Daniel. *Ecosystems of North America: The Everglades and the Gulf Coast*. Tarrytown, NY: Benchmark Books, 2000. An informative look at two unique ecosystems.

Friend, Sandra, and Sandra Downs. *Florida in the Civil War: A State in Turmoil*. Brookfield, CT: Twenty-First Century Books, 2001. A portrait of a conflicted Florida during troubled times.

Gallagher, Jim. *Explorers of the New World: Hernando De Soto and the Exploration of Florida*. New York: Chelsea House, 2000. The first Europeans arrive in Florida.

McCarthy, Kevin M. *Native Americans in Florida*. Sarasota, FL: Pineapple Press, 1999. A general reference source.

Sherrow, Victoria. *Hurricane Andrew: Nature's Rage*. Berkeley Heights, NJ: Enslow Publishers, 1998. A profile of one of Florida's most violent hurricanes.

Siegelson, Kim. *Escape South*. New York: Golden Books, 2000. While many slaves escaped to the North, a large number went south and joined the Seminole nation.

Silverstein, Alvin, et al. *Endangered in America: The Florida Panther*. Brookfield, CT: Millbrook Press, 1997. A nonfiction account of the Florida panther.

Web Sites

▶ Official state web site
www.state.fl.us

▶ Official state capital web site
www.state.fl.us/citytlh

▶ The Florida History Museum online
dhr.dos.state.fl.us/museum

▶ The Florida Natural History Museum online
www.flmnh.ufl.edu

Films

Cohen, Art, and Jonathan Bird. *Endangered Mermaids: The Manatees of Florida*. Boston: Oceanic Research Group, 2001. Learn about these wonderful and endangered creatures.